Poems for Gustav Klimt

First published 2024 by The Hedgehog Poetry Press

Published in the UK by
The Hedgehog Poetry Press
Coppack House, 5
Churchill Avenue
Clevedon
BS21 6QW

www.hedgehogpress.co.uk

Copyright © The Hedgehog Poetry Press 2024

The right of individual contributors to be identified as the author of their work has been asserted in accordance with the Copyright, Designs and Patents Act 1988.

All rights reserved. No part of this publication may be reproduced, stored in or introduced into a retrieval system, or transmitted in any form, or by any means (electronic, mechanical, photocopying, recording or otherwise) without prior written permissions of the publisher. Any person who does any unauthorised act in relation to this publication may be liable for criminal prosecution and civil claims for damages,

9 8 7 6 5 4 3 2 1

A CIP Catalogue record for this book is available from the British Library.

ISBN: 978-1-916830-37-0

Contents

Wendy Goulstone 5
Patricia M Osborne 7
Katrina Moinet 9
Felice Hardy 11
Ceinwen E Cariad Haydon 13
Cassia Stevens 14
Mick Yates 16
Liz Kendall 19
Dawn Gorman 21
Nigel Kent 23
Eileen Carney Hulme 25
Oz Hardwick 26
Jackie Truman 29
Kerry Darbishire 31
Catherine Heighway 32
Christine Macfarlane 34
Marion Ashton 37
Phil Santus 39
Julie De Brito 41
Rebecca Royall 43
Saskia Ashby 45
Roger Waldron 47
Greta Ross 49

WENDY GOULSTONE

The Kiss

He always liked that painting,
the way it sparkles, the richness of it,
the patchwork of their clothes,
the way her head tilts to receive the kiss.

When I visit I bend to kiss him.
He purses his lips ready to receive it.
He used to say 'I love you',
but he's lost the power.
I say it for both of us.

How much longer will he know me?
Soon he will be moved again —
another upheaval, but they need the bed.
I fear the future.

PATRICIA M OSBORNE

The Kiss

Swathed in rich gold, mummified,
he folds his arm around her flowery shroud,
brushes fingertips across her pale cheek.

Eyes closed, she lies transfixed, waits
for the promised kiss on her pinkish lips.

A sweet violet fragrance fills
the metallic vault where time stays still.

KATRINA MOINET

Kuss mit einer Faust

For Emilie, Adele, and other golden women

There's something quite *unheimlich* about your
tightened lids & tilted moon face, toes curled
to grip dear ground; your solid bound to his
expression – glued, in semi-serene dream.

Something *gefährlich* about his stiffened
finger clasp, fists grasping at oval bone
no shimmer space between your split shapes
your swirls boldly blocked by black, silver, gold.

That *etwas unnatürlich* which endures:
a portrait posture held in clutched embrace
disguised trace, facial clues, a light signal
surface tripwires – never step out of frame.

This century's *sinnliche Masse* adores
a brow of smooth acquiescence, gentle
wilting gesture conceals tender splendour
knelt low, as nature's *gift* slips to the abyss.

Title references Florence + The Machine's 'Kiss with a Fist' from the 2009 album 'Lungs'

FELICE HARDY

Swimming with Flowers

Porcelain bodies tinted blue
graceful flight with flowers sweet,
one red as clay, another gold
two heads like buds themselves afloat.

They're racing through the darkness,
in lightening tunnels of their minds,
a boundless leap from canvas
that binds them for eternity.

Seeking freedom where others don't
from the artist's hands and mind,
daubed with oils in a golden frame
expressionism traps, Vienna style.

With reference to Gustav Klimt's 'Water Serpents II' (1907)

CEINWEN E CARIAD HAYDON

It Depends Who's Looking

After Gustav Klimt 'The Three Ages' 1905

Nothing stands still,
permanence, even held in oils,
is illusory. Klimt's women
are moved along by cycles
beyond their control. The seeds
of the elder's bloated belly
are sown within her own mother's womb.
Cascades of curls, grey and auburn,
on two heads,
converse and converge. They meet
in the infant's brunette mop,
held safe in slumbers.
Men may gaze and see this image
as journey from nubile girl to crone
after bairns are born.
My reading differs, I see
the closeness of sisterhood,
old and young depending on each other.
The granddam bends her head in earnest prayer.
Marks of age on her dryer skin
pay homage to a life lived with love,
the young woman's translucent beauty
streams a commitment to her child
who will in different times,
herself, become all three.
The artist paints with honesty
and dignifies
vulnerability, eros, passion and decay.
He backdrops all three figures
with silken textiles
rich with floral beauty,
and brushes into life
protective drapes
against the inevitable coming of night.

CASSIA STEVENS

Response to Gustav Klimt's Die Drei Lebensalter der Frau

All that shimmers is not gold,
a mother's arms that should enfold
hang loosely, empty, by her side,
head bowed with regret, unable to bridge the void.
Her flax-haired daughter, nearby, but worlds apart,
holds her baby skin-close, soft and warm,
eyelids closed in dreaming synchronicity.
Hearts and breasts pressed together in timeless accord,
she mothers to heal the rift
that was her unwanted legacy.

'Die Drei Lebensalter der Frau' - 'The Three Ages of Woman'

MICK YATES

Poem For Gustav Klimt

snakes that resemble

a kaleidoscopic heaven

or a rich tapestry

hanging in a museum

for all to wander by

and marvel at such

glorious textures and colours

such miracles as these

are seldom seen

in this world

and should be savoured

in all their splendour

LIZ KENDALL

Danaë, 1907, Gustav Klimt

Haunch is a word of plenty:
      venison strong with blood and wildness,
      rich for the wealthy palate or poacher.

Gold-touched purple-black fills a corner with gauze like
                  oil rippling on water, slick and choking,
                  like pepper that tingles the air then settles.

Pepper the irritant, catch in the throat:
there must be a muscular squeeze, a release,
there must be there must be...

remember:
pepper and gold were once worth the same,
weighed and measured, pouched in leather.

And you, Danaë, amber-haired girl, you let it all come.
Let it come to you, god-given waterfall falling in gold.

The cup that fills without seeking,
the wine flows to you.

Like the Mint like Fort Knox like the magic box
you open only to become more valuable.

Darling, where is your other hand?
Is there a gleam in your palm?

DAWN GORMAN

Pleasure

For Gustav Klimt, after 'Mohnfeld', 1907

It's a perfect day.
The kind you want to take home with you,
an amulet of summer green against a later dark.
You cut out a small square shape
from a piece of card
and look at the orchard
through the space you've made,
frame your rapture.
The fruit is already golden on the trees,
and beneath, pure colour –
poppies, cornflowers, buttercups,
little dabs of gemstones
you might see against the curve
of a woman's neck,
the softest white of her inner arm.

You lift your brush
to put a line around your thoughts –
landscape to set the eye on fire,
birdsong to bathe the heart,
wild flowers to scent each breath,
and the sweet joy of pears,
once at the bite,
once more at the juice on another's lips.

So here it is, and here it will always be –
a perfect day,
one that knows how gaining pleasure
is the most important thing in life.
And that is all.

NIGEL KENT

Woman in a black feather hat

after Gustav Klimt

She was different
from the others:
those confections
of male fantasies.
Divinities displayed
in all their nakedness
provoking the bull in men,
pictured as tenderness.
Timeless icons
venerated in gold
mounted on walls
to idolise.

She was someone else:
clothes chosen to conceal,
not to flatter or flaunt;
lower lip pressed shut,
not parted in the promise
of a kiss;
eyes averted to avoid
the voyeur's gaze;
and so pale, so slight,
almost inconspicuous,
were it not for that hat,
a nest of crow-black feathers
resting on a head
teeming with ideas,
all chirping for release.

EILEEN CARNEY HULME

Whoever wants to know something about me look carefully at my pictures
you once said. It's difficult to escape your
presence here in Vienna, dear Gustav
and of course I am often forgotten
except perhaps on viewing *The Kiss*.
Who is the woman?
At midnight's deserted hour I stand in
this museum with its hauntings.
And I look carefully, studying myself
momentarily dismissing you.
Some say I never liked this painting, this
Portrait of Emilie Flöge
and that my family refused to display it.
But here it hangs and here I remain by design
in mesmerising shapes, exquisite colours of blue
purple and gold — my needle and thread my voice.
Hand on hip I look back at myself, strong, fearless
daring, much more than a muse.

OZ HARDWICK
Memories of the Dream House

Skimming the surface, a house is a house, is a hauled-up hoard of someone else's memories, daubed at the limits of lawn. It's a clutch of lines sketched round another family's small rituals and small regrets, then dashed with leaves and flowers. Who lives inside these shuttered windows? Who trims the jasmine and honeysuckle that scent the wind that penetrates peeling doors? Behind us, a road or a river, the rush of passing lives that never rest, eyes skimming the surface and missing the details. At our feet, poppies and daisies. At our shoulders, birdsong. At the end of a long day, a fire snaps in a simple hearth, swallowing rituals and regrets. The surface ripples. Births and deaths behind yawning walls, and the scent of remembrance drifts from room to room.

Water Serpents II

Finally, the sky is falling, with fish and flowers, and all the other attributes of popular civic legend. Every dog has had its day and shaken it until it no longer even rattles. The meek inherited the Earth but sold it back to the rich for the price of a bag of burger buns, a couple of tins of tuna, and a scratch card for the chance to win a decent burial. We take comfort in familiar formats, and when the power outs, we gather in candlelit parlours and while away the evenings enacting biblical tableaux of the slaughter of the innocents or Sodom and Gomorrah. And still the sky falls, and when we venture out, we're waist deep in flowers, and the fish are evolving before our eyes into fire-haired sirens who sing the new perfection in voices even dogs can't hear.

JACKIE TRUMAN

Portrait of Fritza Riedler

She sits in a patterned chair
pinned like a pale butterfly.
Expressionless,
looking out at the artist.
Her hands loose and uncertain
questioning the man.
He has arranged her hair,
her clothes, her body.
The choking necklace,
beribboned dress,
cascades of white lace
hide her small frame.
Trapped,
a commission,
a trophy,
another conquest
for the man in the blue robe.
Unfettered by convention
he paints his lover,
the captured woman.

KERRY DARBISHIRE

Emilie Louise Flöge – the forgotten fashion designer

Oil on canvas – Gustav Klimt 1902

What were you thinking, all flushed lips and brambled hair, staring out
at us with strident self-confidence? Such a look – liberated in your blue
patterned dress glittering like stars falling into the curves of The Danube.

Couturière on the bustling Mariahilfer Strasse, leading figure during
the *fin-de-siècle* in Viennese-bohemian spirit alongside Paul Poiret
and later Coco Chanel, tell me, in your blossoming as Klimp's muse,

was it more than simply modelling hour after hour? Often you bled
together in squares and circles, Hungarian and Slavic prints – indulgent
embroidery, floral decorative motifs, and those glints of gold inspired

by the Far East. Your eyes tell me there's something more than his exotic
handling of blue and gold, his gaze in each brush stroke, sensual complexity,
the freedom of silk touching your skin.

CATHERINE HEIGHWAY

Vienna 1950

After 'Portrait of Emilie Flöge' by Gustav Klimt -1902

I stand in front of my portrait
in the Wein Museum   it's quiet
no one knows who I am but may know

this moon face framed by unruly curls
this confident stance with hand on hip
this elongated body that fills the canvas

most will comment on the gown
that skims the floor in the painting
my creation flowing free as a river

the fabric with its purple spirals
blue waves   white dots   gold squares
like a Byzantine mosaic

mother refused the portrait
hated it   the parted lips
flushed cheeks   sensuous outline

I hated it too   he painted me as
an illusion   a gilded beauty
too mystical   too dreamy

these bright eyes saw it all
his liaisons   his illegitimate children
while Viennese society called me *Frau Klimt*

even though he wouldn't marry me
I was his *Lebensmensch*
my name the last word on his lips

Lebensmensch – the most important person in someone's life

CHRISTINE MACFARLANE

Questions for Gustav Klimt

... *To know something about me...*
look carefully at my paintings.

I have looked and I wonder,
what's all this bling, so much
gilding of lily-white bodies?
I look at *The Kiss*. He, bodyless
has her head in a close grip.
Is her hand pulling his away?
Her toes are curled. Is she
enjoying this, Herr Klimt,
under her cloth of gold?
Is there a hint of contempt
for these young, not shown in
The Blind Man or landscapes?
Erotica in gold must sell well.
One perhaps funds the other?

MARION ASHTON
Woman in Gold

Home in on me, you say,
revere the detail and intricacy —
gold on gold, a golden cosmos
adorning my figure. Admire the lines,
spots and curves of my flowing shawl —
the tactile elegance of slippery silk.

Catch wide eyes peering at you
from the body-clutching dress.
Stroke the skin of smooth long arms
and intertwined slim-fingered hands.

Look at my face, you say —
alabaster pale — held high
by the diamond-dotted choker,
my pert red lips, pink-spotted cheeks —
sheer extravagance, assured allure,
owl-eyed opulence and artistry.

PHIL SANTUS

Klimt's women

Who are these apparitions?
Surely not figures from mythology,
they look too modern for that.

They are more like the posturing
of the new wealthy classes,
creating legends of their own.

Their expressions are other-worldly.
They are self-made and ascendent,
telling to us their story.

They live for their aspirations
and glory in their accomplishments,
remote from people's problems,

Gold inlay and skin of pearly white,
these are the sirens of their modern age.
With old forms superseded,
this is the new style of things.

JULIE DE BRITO

Judith by Gustav Klimt, 1901

You lost your head, Holofernes
not once but twice,
and it was just like a little death
when I opened you up
and spilled your wine-hot breath.

You're all mine now, Holofernes
resting your head in my hands
like a sighing lover.
Look how you've uncovered
my golden ascendancy.

I feel for you, Holofernes,
I really do.

REBECCA ROYALL

Amalie

composed
on canvas

incompleteness
filling a frame

no entry number
tattooed
on your unfinished arms

no sharp lines
of starvation

on completed face
no tears

for yourself
your daughter
murdered at Belzec

how can you hang
light

as the lace
you wear

holding such
weight?

SASKIA ASHBY

I become a field

When you are near
I become a field
Of sunflowers
Near Seville
Where the air
Smells of oranges
I grow tall
All my million
Faces tilt and turn
Towards you
Track your path
Across the sky
Until the last
Drop of twilight
When all my million
Sunflowers wait

For your return.

ROGER WALDRON

MisQuoting Gustav Klimt with Jackson Pollock

I was in this bar with a bloke
who said he was Jackson
Pollock and I'd got no reason to
doubt him never seen a photo and
his shoes were covered in paint
and before we got onto other
artists I'd ordered another couple
of fingers of Jack to loosen his tongue
then it began with what you could only
call an onslaught he went on about
art for what seemed like a lifetime
much of which I can't recall but
he did mention Gustav Klimt
and the one with the woman
he thought its title was something
like Judith and the head of Aloofness
then he gave me his thoughts on white
walled tyres and how they looked iconic

GRETA ROSS

Schubert at the Piano

Notes incandesce from his fingers,
three girls, tulip-orange and silver,
sing lieder to candles fizzing gold.

In shadow stands a man half-lit,
eyes deep-set, clipped beard,
could that be Klimt stealing in

to savour the scene soon to be paint?
On canvas his Sirens will shimmer
mirages floating on song.

www.ingramcontent.com/pod-product-compliance
Lightning Source LLC
Chambersburg PA
CBHW041311110526
44590CB00028B/4326